BOATS
on the Move

Willow Clark

WITHDRAWN

PowerKiDS press™

New York

To John, who taught me how to cruise

Published in 2010 by The Rosen Publishing Group, Inc.
29 East 21st Street, New York, NY 10010

First Edition

Editor: Nicole Pristash
Book Design: Kate Laczynski
Photo Researcher: Jessica Gerweck

Photo Credits: Cover, p. 1 © www.istockphoto.com/Brooks Elliot; p. 4 © www.istockphoto.com/ Jordan Shaw; p. 6 Getty Images; pp. 8, 12 Shutterstock.com; p. 10 © Roine Magnusson/ age fotostock; pp. 14–15 Per Breiehagen/Getty Images; p. 16 Courtesy of the Department of Defense; p. 18 © USCG Photo by Joseph P. Cirone; p. 20 Courtesy of Earthrace.net.

Library of Congress Cataloging-in-Publication Data

Clark, Willow.
  Boats on the move / Willow Clark.
      p. cm. — (Transportation station)
  Includes index.
  ISBN 978-1-4358-9336-8 (library binding) — ISBN 978-1-4358-9760-1 (pbk.) — ISBN 978-1-4358-9761-8 (6-pack)
  1. Boats and boating—Juvenile literature. I. Title.
  VM150.C536 2010
  623.82—dc22
                                            2009027410

Manufactured in the United States of America

CPSIA Compliance Information: Batch #WW10PK: For Further Information contact Rosen Publishing, New York, New York at 1-800-237-9932

Contents

Boats are used for many fun things. These boys are jumping off of a boat to go swimming in a lake!

Let's Talk About Boats!

If you have been near a lake, a river, or an ocean, then you have likely seen boats. Boats are small vehicles that are used to move over water. Some boats are used for **cruising** and for water sports. Other boats are built for racing or for use in the military. In fact, there is a type of boat for just about anything you can do on water.

This book will teach you about just a few of the many kinds of cool boats there are, such as speedboats, hydroplanes, and military boats. Put on a life vest and get ready to learn all about these amazing vehicles!

This image shows a group of Native Americans fixing a canoe, or a light boat, in the 1800s. Native Americans generally made canoes out of tree logs.

From Logs to Engines

Throughout human history, people have used boats to travel on water. Early boats were dug out of logs or were made of pieces of wood tied together. Boats were used as far back as 3500 BC, when the Egyptians built big boats to move goods for trade.

Until the 1800s, boats were generally powered in two ways. They were either powered by people rowing them or by the wind. Boats powered by steam engines were invented in the early 1800s. As the century went on, faster and more powerful boats were built. Most of the boats in use today are powered by engines.

This picture shows the starboard side of a speedboat.
Inset: *Here you can see two propellers, which push boats forward in the water.*

All About Boats

Learning boat lingo, or special language, is important to understanding how boats work. The body of the boat is called the hull. Boats float because the hull **distributes** the boat's weight in the water. **Propellers** on the engine push the boat forward, while **rudders** help steer the boat.

The front of the boat is called the bow. The bow has a curved shape, which helps the boat move through the water easily. When you are on a boat and facing the bow, the right side of the boat is called starboard, and the left side is called port. The back part of a boat is called the stern.

Waterskiing, shown here, is a popular sport in which speedboats are used. In this sport, a person wearing skis is pulled behind a speedboat while holding on to a rope.

Built for Speed

One of the most common types of boats is the speedboat. Speedboats are used in races and for riding around on the water. They are generally made of light materials, such as **plastic**.

Some speedboats have an inboard motor, which means that the engine is inside the hull. Other speedboats have an outboard motor, which is a motor on the outside of the boat.

Speedboats are built to go fast. The Skater 36 speedboat can hit speeds of over 180 miles per hour (290 km/h)! It is one of the fastest speedboats in the world.

When a hydroplane boat, such as this one, is planing, only a small part of the boat's hull is touching the water. Pages 14–15: A speedboat moving fast.

Racing Fast

Another fast boat is a hydroplane boat. A hydroplane boat is a one-person motorboat that rides along the **surface** of the water when it hits high speeds. This is called planing. Hydroplane boats are used only in races.

Hydroplane boat races generally take place on lakes. The boats race at speeds of over 70 miles per hour (113 km/h). Hydroplane boats are some of the fastest boats in the world. In 1978, the world water speed record was set by driver Ken Warby. He drove his hydroplane boat, *The Spirit of Australia*, 317 miles per hour (510 km/h)!

INFORMATION STATION

1. One of the world's oldest boats was found in Kuwait in 2002. The boat is believed to be around 7,000 years old.

2. Some of the kinds of boats that people row are called canoes, kayaks, and gondolas.

3. Motorboats can be used for many things other than racing, such as fishing and waterskiing.

4. Boaters can use different gadgets for **navigation**. Before these were invented, people used the Sun and the stars to figure out if their boat was on course.

5 Today, a **Global Positioning System**, or GPS, is a widely used navigational tool for both sea and land. A GPS uses **satellites** to show users where they are.

6 In cities that are near water, police departments often use boats to keep watch and to catch people who have done something illegal.

7 The best way to keep yourself safe while riding on a boat is to wear a life vest. A life vest is a sleeveless jacket that keeps your head and your nose above the water.

A rigid hull inflatable boat, such as this one, has an inflatable tube around its edge. This allows the boat to stay afloat even if the boat takes on a lot of water.

Military Boats

Militaries all around the world use boats. The U.S. military uses boats to help people who are in trouble at sea. It also uses boats to keep the country's waterways and shores safe.

One of the most common types of military boats is the **rigid** hull **inflatable** boat, or RIB. RIBs are made to carry a team, which often includes eight members of the Navy SEAL force and three crew members. The Navy uses these boats to get their members where they need to be quickly. Navy RIBs are around 36 feet (11 m) long, and they can travel up to 52 miles per hour (84 km/h).

18 *This is a U.S. Coast Guard Defender class boat. This boat is used to keep America's coastal waterways safe.*

Boats on the Coast

The Coast Guard is a branch of the U.S. military that looks after America's coasts. The Coast Guard **rescues** boaters and makes sure that no harmful goods or people enter the country.

Coast Guard Defender class boats are used to travel along the coast and to keep watch. These boats can easily make sharp turns, and they travel up to 52 miles per hour (84 km/h). Motor lifeboats, or MLBs, are Coast Guard rescue boats. These boats are built to ride in rough seas. If a motor lifeboat is flipped over during a bad storm, it can turn itself back over!

Earthrace *has three hulls instead of one, as most boats have. The hulls are thin, which allows the boat to move through waves, instead of on top of them.*

One of the coolest boats in the world was built only to break a record using a **renewable resource**. It is called *Earthrace*. *Earthrace* is a speedboat that is powered by biodiesel.

Biodiesel is fuel made from plant matter instead of oil. Unlike oil, biodiesel is a renewable resource, and burning it does not hurt Earth. *Earthrace* can go about 14,913 miles (24,000 km) on just one tank of biodiesel!

In 2008, *Earthrace* set the speed record for a powerboat circling the world. It made the 27,619-mile (44,448 km) trip in 60 days, 23 hours, and 49 minutes.

Boats in Our World

Boats have a long history, but how will they change in the coming years? Biodiesel boats and boats powered by the Sun are being built today. Their inventors hope these boats will help Earth become a healthier place.

Boats are some of the most interesting vehicles in the world because they are used for such different purposes. People use boats to relax on the water, to take part in races, and to keep their country safe. Boats have not only changed the way people enjoy our rivers, lakes, and oceans, but they have also helped make the world a safer place.

Glossary

cruising (KROO-zing) Moving smoothly and easily.

distributes (dih-STRIH-byoots) Spreads something out over a large space.

Global Positioning System (GLOH-bul puh-ZIH-shun-ing SIS-tum) A tool that helps find your location on a map.

inflatable (in-FLAY-tuh-bul) Can be filled with air and expanded.

navigation (na-vuh-GAY-shun) The act of guiding a boat.

plastic (PLAS-tik) Something hard and man-made used to make many things.

propellers (pruh-PEL-erz) Paddlelike parts on an object that spin to move the object forward.

renewable (ree-NOO-uh-bul) Can be replaced once it is used up.

rescues (RES-kyooz) Saves someone or something from harm.

resource (REE-sors) Something that occurs in nature and can be used or sold.

rigid (RIH-jid) Hard.

rudders (RUH-durz) Long boards that stick out from the bottom of a boat to steer the boat.

satellites (SA-tih-lyts) Machines in space that circle Earth and that are used to track weather.

surface (SER-fes) The outside of anything.

Index

Web Sites

Due to the changing nature of Internet links, PowerKids Press has developed an online list of Web sites related to the subject of this book. This site is updated regularly. Please use this link to access the list: www.powerkidslinks.com/stat/boat/